"Megan Fernandes is one of my favorite  the page that I and most other poets can't ... her liberated image and metaphor. All tha... tun-ner, *I Do Everything I'm Told*. The co... love poems like all the best poetry collections are. The pretense of ... past tense of love, and what we do when the little galaxies we build with others start to come apart. Fernandes navigates these spaces with the kind of slick wit and care that love poems require: awareness, eros, and utter abandon. Her first two collections showed us the possibilities for a different kind of poem. *I Do Everything I'm Told* shows us what poetry looks like in the aftermath."

—**ADRIAN MATEJKA**,
author of *Somebody Else Sold the World*

"Beautiful, provocative pleasures, these poems apply a sophisticated intelligence to the most vulnerable and insatiable yearnings. Fernandes degloves traditions of love poetry through her radically adventurous poetry, baring the muscle beneath the skin. Each poem, ungovernable and alive to the contemporary moment, carries forward an original and compelling vision. The result is a brilliant triumph—both poignant and bracing."

—**LEE UPTON**,
author of *The Day Every Day Is*

"In *I Do Everything I'm Told*, we are embraced simultaneously by finality and ambiguity, rules made only to be broken, and in their tesserae lies a beauty that rejects its own existence while reflecting back our own. 'Sometimes, I wonder if I would know a beautiful thing / if I saw it,' Fernandes writes, making of wonder itself a journey beyond the veil where death, violence, and uncertainty herald revision, witness, and love. An incredible book!"

—**PHILLIP B. WILLIAMS**,
author of *Mutiny*

"I love the way this poet celebrates the contradictions of the human condition in poems that are as wise as they are wily. This is a poet whose work displays formal acuity, yes, as but also an expansive depth of play. This collection serves and swerves, sings and swings."

—**TARFIA FAIZULLAH**,
author of *Registers of Illuminated Villages*

I DO
EVERYTHING
I'M TOLD

I DO EVERYTHING I'M TOLD

poems

MEGAN FERNANDES

TIN HOUSE / PORTLAND, OREGON

Epigraph from Lauren Berlant and Lee Edelman, "Sex without Optimism,"
in *Sex, or the Unbearable*, Copyright © 2014, Duke University Press.
All rights reserved. Reprinted by permission of the publisher.

First US Edition 2023
Printed in the United States of America

Manufacturing by Kingery Printing Company
Interior design by Beth Steidle

Library of Congress Cataloging-in-Publication Data

Names: Fernandes, Megan, author.
Title: I do everything I'm told : poems / Megan Fernandes.
Other titles: I do everything I am told
Description: Portland, Oregon : Tin House, [2023]
Identifiers: LCCN 2023003251 | ISBN 9781953534880 (paperback) |
ISBN 9781953534965 (ebook)
Subjects: LCGFT: Poetry.
Classification: LCC PS3606.E7328 A6 2023 | DDC 811/.6—dc23/eng/20230130
LC record available at https://lccn.loc.gov/2023003251

Tin House
2617 NW Thurman Street, Portland, OR 97210
www.tinhouse.com

DISTRIBUTED BY W. W. NORTON & COMPANY

2 3 4 5 6 7 8 9 0

For the restless

CONTENTS

I

Tired of Love Poems / 3

Letter to a Young Poet /4

Dinner with Jack / 5

Paris Poem without Clichés / 6

Drive / 7

Semiotics / 8

Orlando / 11

How to Have Sex in Your Thirties (or Forties) / 12

Winter / 14

Space Cowboi / 16

Shanghai / 18

The Trial / 20

Companion / 21

II
Sonnets of the False Beloveds with One Exception
or Repetition Compulsion

Shanghai Sonnet / 24

Brooklyn Sonnet / 26

Los Angeles Sonnet / 28

Lisbon Sonnet / 30

Palermo Sonnet / 32

Paris Sonnet / 34

Philadelphia Sonnet / 36

Wandering Sonnet / 38

Diaspora Sonnet / 39

III

Do You Sell Dignity Here? / 45

I'm Smarter than This Feeling, but Am I? / 48

In Death, We Met in Scotland / 49

Catskills / 50

Fuckboy Villanelle / 53

Rilke / 54

Too Much Eliot / 56

Get Your Shit Together and Come Home / 57

Reunion / 59

Masculinity / 61

Pound and Brodsky in Venice / 62

Debt / 63

Phoenix / 66

Sagittarius / 67

IV

I Do Everything I'm Told / 71

May to December / 72

Autumn in New York, 2020 / 73

The Poet and the Nurse / 74

The First Outing / 76

Beggars and Choosers / 77

Retrospect / 78

Magical Realism in America /80

Company, Company / 82

Sonnet for the Unbearable / 83

On Your Departure to California / 84

Malaika / 85

Love Poem / 86

Notes / 88

Acknowledgments / 89

I

"Sit where the light corrupts your face."

—GWENDOLYN BROOKS,
In the Mecca

TIRED OF LOVE POEMS

But we never tire of them, do we?
We wish to worship more than just each other.
We put a god first, sometimes a tree,
write a sonnet to a bird in the black
of night or offer a light to a stranger
and not call it love. But it is. To pull
out a chair is more than manners.
What we tire of is that we never tire of it.
How it guts us. How it fails, then reappears.
Because what is the bird compared to you?
The bird is replaced each morning.
You approach on a red bike in summer
and the poem takes shape. I entitle it
anything but Love, anything but what it is.

LETTER TO A YOUNG POET

If you haven't taken the Amtrak in Florida, you haven't lived. At 2:00 a.m., seven months into the pandemic, I'm looking up where Seamus Heaney died. It was Blackrock Clinic overlooking the sea and I wonder, sometimes, what is my thing with the Irish, but if the white kids can go to India for an epiphany, maybe it's fine that I go to Ireland. Don't read Melanie Klein in a crisis. She's depressing and there are alternatives. Like Winnicott or a lobotomy. Flow is best understood through Islamic mysticism or Lil Wayne spitting without a rhyme book, post-2003. To want the same things as you age is not always a failure of growth. A good city will not parent you. Every poet has a love affair with a bridge. Mine is the Manhattan and she's a middle child. Or the Sea Link in Mumbai, her galactic tentacles whipping the starless sky. When I say *bridge*, what I mean is goddess. People need your ideas more than your showmanship. L.A. is ruining some of you. All analysis is revisionist. Yellow wildflowers are it. It's better to be illegible, sometimes. Then they can't govern you. It takes time to build an ethics. Go slow. Wellness is a myth and shame transforms no one. You can walk off most anything. Everyone should watch anime after a heartbreak. Sleep upward in a forest so the animal sees your gaze. I think about that missing plane sometimes and what it means to go unrecovered. Pay attention to what disgusts you. Some of the most interesting people have no legacy. Remember that green is your color and in doubt, read Brooks. In the end, your role is to attend to the things you like and ask for more of it: Bridges. Ideas. Destabilization. Yellow tansy. Cities. The wild sea. And in the absence of recovery, some ritual. In the absence of love? Ritual. Understand that ritual is a kind of patience, an awaiting and waiting. Keep waiting, kitten. You will be surprised what you can come back from.

DINNER WITH JACK

A couple go scuba diving and by accident,
get left behind in the water. The boat roars off.
And there they float, in full gear and disbelief,
tanks low on air, stranded in a seamless blue,
deciding if they can survive until the next day, which,
of course, they cannot, because the average person
can only tread four hours without a life jacket.
The couple bicker: *Why did we go on this vacation?*
Why did you choose this company? Why did I choose you?
And even when it's too late, with fatigue building
in their arms and waves buoying their bodies
like a whipped dessert, they make their case of a soulmate
gone wrong. Because a real love story would never end like this.
Eventually, the couple must choose their deaths.
One removes their suit and slips into hypothermic sleep,
and the other cuts and spills blood to entice a shark.
Both choices tell us something about our protagonists,
who are maybe not even our protagonists since
they are so bitter one cannot fully root for them.
See, the logic of a couple is like a Beckett play.
Facing the end, you don't want someone with you
for comfort. You want someone with you to blame.
Jesus, I reply, and cut my steak like a heart.

PARIS POEM WITHOUT CLICHÉS

There are two sides to every story, except this one.
We're no longer babes in the forest with an axe to grind.
We're so behind the times, we blow gaskets,
we pick bones to break the ice. Crazy as a loon,
we cry the river together, cut a rug
around the killed cat who needed to die, I guess,
for wanting to know more. We got your knickers
in a twist and dropped like flies. As beautiful
as the day is light, which is not so long. Give or take
ten summer hours. We went dutch at dinner
and rose early to eat worms. There was a lone swan
stranded in the canal, swimming in stupid circles,
searching for her better half who abandoned ship.
She had an orange mouth. Absence makes a heart
of thorns. Someone chucked trash in the
green-with-envy waters, so close to her feathers
she panicked to keep herself preened, pristine, in case
her faint heart got lost in the shuffle, again.
What do you want. It was Paris and full of grief.
A last hurrah. A lost cause. A Lord willing.
I'd beg to differ. I wasn't born yesterday.

DRIVE

I walk into a record store on Christmas Eve and The Cars are playing so, of course,
I think of you. In therapy, I learn words and box three days a week and read Russel Brand's

book about being fucked and for months, cut out drinking and apply to Divinity school
and examine my life and the impossibility of *you* and *I* and how *I* is a mirror and *you*

is nothing but a projection of *I* and I did try, honestly. I recited clichés when language failed
and let my self-helping heart run ravenous at a buffet of cheap routines and then

came armed, one day, with my ancestors who had lived through revolutions and ships
raging at their shores and they, too, shrugged at me, so I blamed sexuality and childhood

and made every target an easy one, just to make it make sense, but it wouldn't fit.
Nothing fit. And my friends said words about history and power, and I wanted the pain

to be ideological but it was too easy, and nobody admits that ideology can envelop
almost anything and therefore, is bad form. I gave up. It was an angelic state, a surrender

to a belief that *you* and the *I* was a unity that could return one home if home
were a pair of blue stars in devoted orbit, seen as one bright pulse from earth,

away from the brute facts of living. But home is not two suns. There is no home
and nothing to return to, just a series of shadows, partial signs of presence: a flickering.

I say things and then unsay them. It was love. It was not love. It is raining. It is not raining.
Contradictions are a sign we are from god. We fall. We don't always get to ask why.

SEMIOTICS

I went to the Rockaways
to look for dolphins,

saw three, and assigned each of them
a meaning. I called it a sign.

This is what I do. Find a noun,
usually an animal, and give it

an intervention in my life.
And if there is sudden rain?

Even better. I don't believe
in coincidences

when the sea and sky talk
in tandem. That's fate.

Last year, instead
of going to rehab,

my friend booked a trip
to the Maldives

and asked me to join him.
He put the whole thing

on his credit card, and did it
the minute we got home

from Presbyterian on 75th
while an orange ID bracelet

still spun on his wrist
like the Wonder Wheel.

What should I say to him?
That I admire his audacity

to be ill? That he knows
to be ill is natural

given the state of this world,
and how is everyone

not ill, not overdosing
on the night? Because

the nukes are coming.
Our optimism

is not enough
to make it not so.

Our optimism is all we have.
Well, that and beauty.

He always says to me:
Megan, beauty doesn't need a metaphor.

He asks if I will stop him.
I shrug. Only he knows

what can save us
and anyways,

the interventions
I believe in

are not earthly.
I mean, he's got

Coney Island
on his wrist.

One must look for signs
to believe in them.

ORLANDO

The few weeks I was pregnant, whenever people asked
how are you, meg? I'd answer, *oh ya know... with child*
which I thought was dead funny. I don't think about it now
except sometimes in a fitness class surrounded by women
trying to shed baby weight and I make the calculations
(he'd be about fourteen by now) and then I look at myself
in the class mirror while women squat and lift their legs
and think, wow! I look so good for having a fourteen-
year-old and then I'd think again, how if he were a reality,
I'd say it all the time and embarrass him in front of his
school friends and for some reason, I think he'd be
a drummer and wear green. I have no regrets,
but I wonder if he's waiting in the sky somewhere
or doing blow in another dimension where he's a rocker
and very much flesh. I don't believe in kin by blood,
but I believe poems can give form to the formless,
that one can resurrect roads not taken in a line
and give it a name. *It's a novel by Virginia Woolf,* I'd say
and rattle on and he'd wave me off but maybe read it
one day in college and think about his young mother
who wanted to be a writer and what she might have had
to give up in order to raise him at twenty-three.
He'd write me a song. He'd title it with my name.

HOW TO HAVE SEX IN YOUR THIRTIES (OR FORTIES)

Only way is to fuck
like you're stalling

the body's departure
from doing

what bodies will do:
end. Call it back

from its route
to extinction.

Tether
it to its own

underbelly, the land
of living. Speak

its basement desire.
If you can do that,

well, then
you've done a thing.

Young sex
misunderstands metaphor.

To the young,
the dying

of the light
is mere abstraction.

in the dead cold. I have
two cats in New York

and not so much loneliness.
Still, I prepare for their deaths,

but who knows, I may go first.
Sorry, but I'm like this in winter.

My composure an evergreen with
the settled world that keeps settling.

I trek the season.
I arrange the dance of blooms,

room to room, and keep
my small perimeter fed and alive.

We tread to March
like soldiers, like sailors tossed

into navy tides, into
wave white, and who,

spotting land, at last,
grow gills at its sight.

SPACE COWBOI

When they ask
to describe your relationship
you reply, playfully,

do you mean cosmically?
and they say no.
They did not mean cosmically.

In Shanghai, I go to the gym
and fall apart in the locker room
surrounded by bright limbs

untying hair buns, sweat
swept off foreheads.
No one really speaks English

or pretends not to while
I ugly cry before a class
that I learn, too late,

is a K-pop dance routine
and so there I am, hopping along
on one leg to a song

that let's face it, is pretty good.
Next time we meet,
it will be on Saturn's highway

of ice. I will say *hey, over here!*
and you'll hop a few rings, plop
down in ski pants, skid off the side

a bit. It will be galactically comic.
You will say sorry about those years
but we'll be too distracted by

Jupiter's nearby ocean
and the multi-colored swirls
galloping on solar racetracks.

I tell you about a French poet
who described the universe
as eternally undressing

out of an infinite gown
and you gasp before
we both go quiet. Out here,

we spin and tell jokes
and while I rehearse
K-pop for you

on a thawing moon,
how can it be that
on Earth, we are nothing?

SHANGHAI

I fell in love many times these months
with certain evenings,
the city awash in green Neptune light.
When I was low, I was low.
And the city welcomed it, wrestled
a steady heat from my melancholy.
To be *shanghaied* once meant
to be kidnapped against your will
during a shortage of sailors.
Some were forced to sign with guns to their temples.
Others, beat unconscious, woke
to the wide roaring sea, ready to serve.
It was violent. Today, the bright plazas
speed us into manic dream,
the kind where you know
your executioner is coming
and we all get high
on the fluorescence and doom.
This is a place where I've let people down.
But the penance is different.
Not like New York with her sad gargoyles.
Instead, Shanghai has her young, surveilling moonlight.
Outside, a wild and holy river runs full of tanks
and neon boats peppered below a bulbous skyline.
I fed a cat here. And named her.
Creaturely orange, she disappeared on Hankou Road.
It broke up my whole day. I had that small burst of fantasy
of our life together, me and her,
a new origin story that keeps repeating.
It says: here, here, here. An eternal present that keeps loss at bay.
That is the trick of this city. It looks like a weird hope,
the human species struck by a wondrous asymmetry.
There is a dimension where the cat stays.

Where I stay, too. There is a version
where the world goes uncrushed,
and instead my beloveds multiply,
and with them, their laughters.
We all wake to simultaneous dawns
breaking over Hong Kong and Nairobi,
Guatemala City and Madrid.
When one beloved says good morning,
another says, good morning.
And for another, maybe it is still night.
Here it comes again. Night.
It starts over, but this time
we have tails and survive.
We come when called.

THE TRIAL

Let me begin
with my vices

which are too many
to name

and not as
salacious

as they used
to be.

I sit with
three bouquets

of birthday flowers
to see

which one
dies first

and then
scrutinize

the beloved
who must be

voted off.
Who does this.

How boring
to accumulate love

only
to test it.

COMPANION

"He couldn't improve me unless he killed me."

—RIMBAUD

There are only
two deliriums.
You know the ones.

Rock-bottom
was once
a mining term and then,

meant to mean
a salt-of-the-earth type
like a "bedrock politician."

But a smart person knows
there's nothing
at the end of the world.

Nothing at the bottom
of the pit.
We are repeat offenders

trying to disprove
a bad truth.
To reinvent

the sub-earth,
which is another word
for hell.

Rimbaud wrote
A Season in Hell
after Verlaine

nearly
killed him.
They tried to make it work,

but kept crashing.
No one wins
when they pick

the arch rebel
with bad blood.
Verlaine was sentenced

to hard labor
for two years
and Rimbaud

trafficked arms.
I'd like to see
a Viking

on the hill.
The mind
wanders.

There's nothing
at the bottom
but a view.

II

Sonnets of the False Beloveds
with One Exception

OR

Repetition Compulsion

"Eros is a verb."

—ANNE CARSON,
Eros the Bittersweet

SHANGHAI SONNET

I cast beloveds. I kill them off, too,
because the muse is mostly a bloodless tool.
A plot device. Don't take it personally.
A device isn't personal, but my blue wound
plus yours? It could be exquisite in the right
weather, in the right city. Under a moonless
Pudong, we drag ourselves into twilight, fresh
from a club where everyone, decked in neon,
forgets how to read the sky. I love when you
can't tell if a storm has gone or will soon arrive.
When the sky refuses dawn. Protests time.
It rains, and on cue, you skid and skin your knee.
You bleed. I neglect it. Neglect to inspect it.
I am young and nothing is sacred yet.

I cast

        mostly

     Don't take it

            blue

  It could be

           a

   drag   twilight

     everyone

forgets   when

  a

   sky

rains and   you

    neglect Neglect

    and nothing

BROOKLYN SONNET

You are young and nothing is sacred yet.
Ready to spar, circling the ring, you flirt
with your feet. Gucci kicks. Your dumb face.
You smile like a pink fluorescent sign. I throw left.
I miss. We miss each other. We like Miami
but prefer Manhattan. She's more dramatic.
We are separated by a river, some bridges.
We make chicken. Mango chutney. We plunge
into all that is restless. We're too fast.
Faster than time. I call you about Venus.
Hottest planet, dense as fuck. And did you know,
Da Vinci only made, like, fifteen paintings?
I know how much you dig genius and exceptions.
And someone who breaks a rule to love you.

nothing is sacred
Ready
your feet
smile like a pink
                other
                        more
                                bridges
        chicken
            all that   fast
                time
                            did you know
                    like
I know
        who breaks

LOS ANGELES SONNET

In love, the rules are meant to be broken.
In role-play and foreplay, I break character
and make things as unsexy as possible.
I'm the coy babysitter. You're the dad.
I ask: *How's it going at the geophysical
mining plant?* You struggle to be convincing
as a fake engineer, which has nothing
to do with our script or this dumb city.
I read Freud's book on jokes and analyze
my need to make a stage of every bit.
On the 101, a cop pulls me over in a fit
and my hands balloon on the wheel like a Sartre
play. Like *La Nausée*. He thinks I'm a wise guy.
Or worse, only sees the actress before him.

                    and   character
        and   things
I'm   coy
ask
                            to be convincing
as
                                this dumb
            book   jokes
my need
                    pulls me
                        like
                    I'm   wise   .

Or worse

LISBON SONNET

What is worse than an actress no one believes?
A priest who has to pretend he isn't who he is.
In the city of hills, yellow light dipping
between begonias, I ask you how you hear God
and once you are sure I'm not mocking you,
you describe a vibration. Kneeling at the altar,
I wonder if you're in this for femme Jesus,
Catholicism's gaudy drama, its nudes and thorns.
At night, I eye the Tagus. We talk about
what we must disguise for our families
to survive. Poet and priest. Our non-futures.
Our lies. Sometimes we got so angry at our moms.
They would just shrug and sigh. Say: *My darling,*
nobody told me how to raise a dark child.

                                        no one
          who has to pretend
          In the city
                    I ask   God
                         I'm not mocking
                                        at the altar
                                             Jesus
          gaudy   nudes
                         We talk about
                                   our families
                              Our non-futures
                                   our moms
                                   My darling
          nobody told me

PALERMO SONNET

Nobody tells you how to raise a dark child.
Even Cronus sent his son underwater
because all origins are first strung in myth
and bottomless disappointment. In a street
blackout, we light candles while teenage boys
break into our house just so we know they can
enter whenever they want. Nothing is stolen.
You pour orange rossa and ask what I think
of your hometown. It feels like a proposal.
That night, sailing in a wild storm with Icarus
to our left, you show no fear. You scare men
and gods and joke all women pay for the sins of
fathers, even if they aren't our fathers or sins.
You insist bad weather is a gift. Rain gathers in.

how to raise a   child
        underwater
    first   in
  disappointment   a
black   light
     we know
     Nothing
     and ask
home
  in a wild
     fear   men
     pay
     our fathers
insist

PARIS SONNET

Bad weather is a gift. Rain gathers in
Buttes-Chaumont where I sink stones into
pools of mirrored water spotting the park sand.
I used to beat women, you tell me.
Your face, open, like a lion. It took me too
long to realize that people who read Marx can
also beat women. You are rough just once.
Bruised wrist. We fought on the street.
A child watched under a green awning.
That was the era of violence. And it was
over fast because you knew you were
an experiment. *I am your goddamn slum
experiment*, you laughed. *Your criminal.*
No. Just the cruelest person I have loved.

                              a gift   gathers
                                      into
                                   the park
          I used to   you tell me
                                a lion
                                  who read
                                                    once
                                        on the street
                                  under a green
                      era
              fast
      an experiment
      experiment
      No   the   person I   loved

PHILADELPHIA SONNET

The cruelest person we love is the first.
In triage, they ask what happened.
My sister and I sit still, wait for a revelation.
A third, unnamed party is slow to say:
Three punches. Closed fist. Straight to the head.
I lose fifteen pounds in a few months
and everyone says how good I look except
that boy in Paris. The terrible one.
We sat at a bar. Don't you ever eat?
A poet does not have enough mercy
for all the people who really need it.
I love the word triage because of tri-
Triangles. Tridents. I fall hard in pairs.
I cast beloveds. I kill them off, too.

                                        first
                    ask what happened
                        wait   a revelation
                            is slow
                                    the
                                    few months
                                    look
                                    terrible
                                            eat
                                            mercy
                                            need
                    the word   because
                            I fall
                                        too

WANDERING SONNET

The cruelest person we love is the first.
Bad weather is a gift. Rain gathers in.
Nobody tells you how to raise a dark child.
What is worse than an actress no one believes?
In love, the rules are meant to be broken.
You are young and nothing is sacred yet.
I cast beloveds. I kill them off, too.
I am a beloved. I keep mine, too.
You are old and everything matters.
In love, there are no rules to begin with.
Everyone is an actress and is to be believed.
There is no such thing as a dark child.
It rarely rains. When it does, it flows.
The first person we love is just that: first.

DIASPORA SONNET

I cast mostly, don't take it blue, it could be a drag twilight,
everyone forgets when a sky rains and you neglect, neglect and nothing
is sacred, ready your feet smile like a pink other, more bridges, chicken,
all that fast time, did you know like I know, who breaks and character,
and things, I'm coy, ask to be convincing as this dumb book jokes, my need
pulls me like I'm wise or worse, no one who has to pretend, in a city, I ask
God, I'm not mocking, at the altar, Jesus, gaudy nudes, we talk about
our families, our non-futures, our moms, my darling, nobody told me
how to raise a child, underwater, first in disappointment, a black
light, we know nothing and ask home in a wild fear, men pay, our fathers
insist, a gift gathers into the park, I used to, you tell me, a lion who read
once on the street under a green era, fast, an experiment, experiment, no,
the person I loved first, ask what happened, wait, a revelation is slow the few
months look terrible: eat, mercy, need, the word, because I fall, too.

I cast   I kill

       we drag

    I love   you can't
                                       you skid
You bleed I neglect   I am

            You are
                           you flirt

          You smile   I throw
          I miss We miss   We like

           We are
       We make   We plunge
                   We're
        I call
                you know

        I know you love

       I break

I'm   You are
I ask
    You struggle

       I read

      I get
    I tell

I am

I ask   you are   I'm
you describe   I wonder   you're
                                                                          I eye
We talk   we must
                                            I got   I tell

                                                    we light
                              we know
              You pour   I think

you show   You scare
                              You insist

                                            I sink
                        I used   you tell

              You are   We fought

        you knew   I am   you
laughed   I have

    we love   I sit

              I lose
        I look   We sat   you
        eat
              I love   I fall   I cast
I kill

III

"Subjects are not usually shocked to discover their incoherence or the incoherence of the world; they often find it comic, feel a little ashamed of it, or are interested in it, excited by it, and exhausted by it too."

—LAUREN BERLANT,
Sex, or the Unbearable

DO YOU SELL DIGNITY HERE?

Do you know what aisle
they sell dignity,
I say to the store clerk
on University Avenue.
It is a cold October,
Frank Ocean's "moon river"
croons in my head
and earlier that day
I lay flat in the bathtub
like a wild infant, shower
pouring, thinking
of that Dickinson poem
where she says
a bomb upon the ceiling
is an improving thing—
steam gathering in celestial
curls and I imagine bombs
fizzing out gas and me,
radioactive with love.
At the grocery store, I ask
where they sell dignity
and when the clerk says
sorry, what did you say?
I explain
that I am looking
for dignity,
having lost so much
in the last year
and was wondering
if it were neatly placed
by the baking powder
or perhaps refrigerated
with the perishables

given its fragile shelf life
and yes, I really did ask this
partly because I was being funny
and trying to make a friend
but also, I would have taken
a hug
or any acknowledgment
that I am a person
who can laugh at myself
despite walking
with that odd angle
of defeat.
Children have no dignity
and I really admire that about them.
I love their ruthless response
to injustices, their desire to feed
birds in the park.
To grieve the sea.
Their right to be tired
in public.
Do you sell dignity here?
I ask one last time,
and then tell him
how it went down,
how I had lost mine
in Bushwick of all places
near a building covered in glass
and white girl gentrifiers
having their white girl epiphanies—
such bad coming-of-age trash,
jesus, all my parents' sacrifices for this?
For what?
Is this why I came here from Africa?
they would say over my flat body,
hopefully in the shape of a shrug.
I am undignified.
I prey on fluorescent light.

I enter through the automatic door
of grocery stores with royal glide,
feetless into an even white.
I greet peaches and bawdy
cauliflower, nod to the pink
packets of sweeteners
and wrapped meat thighs.
I am drawn to the milks
and oblong fruit, dent a red
Campbell's can of soup.
I want everything
as cheap and damaged
as this feeling.
When they go low, we go high,
a president's wife said.
I go low some days.
I go so low, you cannot tell me
from the animals we sell.
From the hard grain
my body has become.

I'M SMARTER THAN THIS FEELING, BUT AM I?

I watch your film about fisting: orifice as cave,
as grave, as starlit wormhole dug in space.
You're obsessed by interiority.
By the drunk shipwreck of it. By our inside rivers
so alien, we might as well call them Sweden or Pluto or 1973
and what's the difference, all of them are out of reach.
I know we're both smarter than this feeling
because we have talked about desire and her little games.
I cry easily as I watch. You're old school.
You want what O'Hara wanted, I think, which is a kind of boundlessness
that won't kill anyone. Edging. You don't believe in bodies.
Everyone is dust, condensed by circumstances.
You see what I was before I was a was. An am.
What's your thing with smut, I ask.
You say it's not smut, it's a love story.
To be taken apart is as important as being put together.
Near-annihilation reminds you of a limit
and ask yourself, who do you trust at your limit?
At a party last night in Chinatown, I invent you
walking through the door. It is warm and I smoke
a cigarette on the balcony. Everyone is a producer
and talking about Kathy Acker and what would I say
if I could? That I want our years to keep meeting.
I don't want 1973 or a failed planet or even Sweden.
Instead of saying this, I ask about your film.
We put the art between us because the art exists
and we do not. This is called sublimation.
We puppet our meat in the grey twilight
of the real world and I pretend
I'm not speaking to Time.

IN DEATH, WE MET IN SCOTLAND

Black beach, tides wild upon us,
the waters carried stunned crabs
to the shores. I knew it could not be earth
by their features and we, too, were distorted
by afterlife. But I held your hand.
Or what I think is a hand.
And you smell like your mother
and it returns, the velvet livingness—present
tension, fights we have on streets,
the red light of an Italian fair
where I rob drinks off drunks and everything
is carnivorous and lit. Our meals. Dancing,
when you get low with boys and I laugh,
room wet with joy at your nerve and swag.
You are now synonymous
with the city, synonymous with symphony,
and so it makes sense to meet
here in solemn asphalt, in death.
I touch what I think is your hand
in the afterlife and recall the story
of your mom, newly divorced,
tucking you into bed on New Year's Eve
in Oregon. Your little brother, too.
You choked imagining her lonely countdown
and how you had slept so well
through her despair.

CATSKILLS

I see a shooting star
and don't
make a wish.

Is this fucking Buddhism,
I ask Dan,
who is passed out

in the grass to my right.
He has an app
that shows a giraffe

in the sky.
A gladiator. Mars.
Yesterday,

I stalked
rabbit tracks
in the snow

until I felt the animal
didn't want
to be found.

I don't want
anything
except Zoloft

but stop short
of ingesting.
I am so controlled

this year.
I fuck no one.
I don't drink

myself
into any emergency.
I pass on acid.

I do a little blow.
Tonight,
I bow to a choir

of trees, a majestic
grove of evergreens
who feed

nightly
on stars.
I like you, I say

to a Douglas fir,
which is a joke
because I like

no one
and can't remember
that feeling,

the one like
awaiting
your lover's figure

in a polaroid
to emerge.
I am an '80s myth.

I go
to basketball games
on Christmas,

and eat Chinese
and worry
over all the Catherines

I know.
I thought
the rabbit print

was a bear's at first
because
I'm a city kid

and an idiot.
There was panic
and then

disappointment
that
it belonged

to a body so slight
when
I just want

to be dwarfed
by everything
these days.

FUCKBOY VILLANELLE

See, I've heard it all before
so now, I don't court doom.
I don't break no more.

My own dry, tired score
of notes? Me-as-perfect-groom?
Well, I had done it all before.

I've floated to hell's shore
with the same watery tune.
I've broken many more,

with gifted harp, worn
from use. But Eurydice's tomb
was lousy with my amours,

and they mused, armored
my girl with indifferent blooms.
Until Eurydice said: *no more.*

She didn't turn back to Hades's door.
Not all descent is doom.
Down there, she heard it all before.
And I break no one. No more.

RILKE

"Already she was root."

—RILKE
Orpheus. Eurydice. Hermes

No one in history has ever
been as smart as their husband.
I think of the myths

where men drown and women sit
in the waiting rooms
of the underworld.

See, I think Orpheus knew.
Had always planned to turn back
and homegirl knew, too.

That's a kind of smart.
To know what you know.
To know what your man can and will do

and how it will be later told.
I prefer your kind of smart,
my friend said, by which she means

dumb joy. Hey, it's true. I flip
Hades' den and get people in a room.
I'm good at a party and even better

at dead ends. When I lose a job
at a women's college to a dude,
I mourn in grey silk for days,

play Blanche and feign distress, wander
with cigarette holes in my dress.
You know, for character. To impress.

To make sure I'm convincing enough
to be overlooked. Once, my students
got locked in a room, and I jumped

from a window to let them out.
What mama energy, one student said
and I gave her a C. Baby, I'm Circe.

I hold down the island.
I don't drown my own men in the sea.
I tidy up the underworld, and down here

there's a tunnel to hell
where we wave, each to each.
We bury waterlogged peaches, deep.

We refuse to die in this underneath.
When the detective breaks in and asks
which way he went, I take a drag or sip.

I pivot, indifferent. I curtsey, ankles in check.
I know how to turn around.
I know who waits in this clockless eternity

and who is allowed to drown.

TOO MUCH ELIOT

I only listen to Dinah, now.
Also, Belafonte.
Optimism plus despair

is the soup of our time.
No hope here. No sea.
Some degraded trees

and always a map
that wants to become
something else.

I wouldn't know
a limit unless I hit
an ocean. I stand

dumbfounded when
earth's lip meets the sea.
There are songs

I can't listen to anymore.
I say it's because
of the war. Or the plague.

Easier to blame
the world falling apart
than to say it's you.

Only a rookie admits
the source of pain.
Instead, I rage. I fade.

GET YOUR SHIT TOGETHER AND COME HOME

High on a beach in Miami, I once asked my friends
whether the sun or moon was closer to the earth
and they both looked at me like I was an idiot
and said to never tell anyone I had asked that question aloud.
Kind of like the time I briefly thought I met Spike Lee
at an event and asked him what he did for a living
after saying I was a poet because I did not
recognize him right away and then
I was embarrassed and also wearing a pink jumpsuit
that made me look like a walking salmon. I'm bad at faces,
but I mean, obviously it is the moon or we'd be burnt up by now.
And obviously it was Spike Lee. I am a fish
out of water sometimes, trying to remember
which celestial body is closest. The only tattoo
I got was from a guy named Fish in Portugal
at thirty-five because that was the age
I learned what I could live with forever
and what I could not live without.
With his ink gun halfway in me, I asked,
why do they call you Fish and he said, *because I'm a drunk.*
The tattoo is a word in Sicilian: *ARRICAMPATI,*
which means, loosely, get your shit together
and come home to me, a perfect middle-aged tattoo,
and also what a mother says to a kid who is playing
out in the street too long or what a wife says
to her drunk husband who keeps ordering rounds
at the bar. Exasperation is part of its spell.
I got it with a friend whom I hadn't seen in a year
because of the virus and now, when she's bouncing
from one city to the next, passing out in a hotel in Seoul
and calling to show me the scar on her forehead, I yell,
just pick a place, jesus, I mean, pick a life,

get your shit together and come home to me and she laughs
and says I am one to talk since I am usually the one
on the run, moving so fast I cannot even tell
when I'm facing a legend or how close
the moon has always been by my side.

REUNION

Morning clocks in and the ancient white of Venice
dresses into day. I put on the Fugees in a damp church

with Madonnas swelling, welled in humidity,
and I still have nausea from the plane

where I took up a whole row and stared
at the seatbelt sign glowing, imagining the underbelly

of the bird, coated in a buttery trans-Atlantic moon.
I haven't seen you in a year and now, when I do,

I get jumpy, make us stop into church after church
as we watch the green water churn against stone.

Venice has no streetwear, I say, everyone here looks
like a widow. It always looks like a Sunday.

Really, I'm being defensive about dressing
like an American so I stick hard to stereotypes.

When we get to your apartment, you wash tomatoes,
water rushing on your hands, directly into the sink.

You spit a small harmless seed as we sit on stools
in the lime kitchen and eat them whole. Plum bodies

so fragrant, they make me cry and here I am,
tearing over tomatoes, jetlagged, lagging, delaying

everything, with at least three churches in view.
We're surrounded by time and god.

It makes children of all of us.
And I am not a stupid child.

Before I left, I gathered my breath and for what?
Some grand gesture. No. We keep our heads down.

We study the feet of medieval saints. We make small talk
against the big year of our absence from each other.

MASCULINITY

Of what are you afraid? Not a bomb. In Dar es Salaam the men,
with guns as long as arms, bent under the car to check
for a ticking and you did not even flinch. Not of snow,
when in New Hampshire, a white storm blanketed
the car in minutes and the highway transformed into
a blinding afterlife, skid red, and sightless sounds of metal colliding.
Not of dark, when the motorcycle's headlight burned out
in the dead of night as we wound down a volcano's steep body,
the road's rocky jaw dropping to a rough sea, the free fall inches
from our feet. We fought. Years later, you said
the difference between the two of us was that I always
thought someone was coming to save me.
You said, Meg, if you pull over to the side of the volcano,
an angel will be dispatched, a donkey and a husband and a stable will appear.
If you stop the car in the blizzard, three wise men show up.
If your face moves when they search for bombs, you aren't mistaken for one.
You said, no one is coming to save me.
You said, I save myself.

> I said, okay.
> I said, if you are the bomb then I am the bait.
> I said, if I am saved by three wise men, what will this cost me?
> Will I have to drop to my knees?
> Because no man gives salvation away for free.

But I said none of this. Because when I heard *no one is coming to save me*,
I held you close like a good woman. Like all the women before me
who know what destroys and remakes, and what is destroyed in the remaking.

POUND AND BRODSKY IN VENICE

I don't even dig Pound. But in a sunk cemetery in a sinking city
poets stick together. Brodsky is buried two feet away and for him

I leave an MTA card and a wild daisy, mutter about the metaphors
of transit, tell him how last night, with my feet dangling off the shoreline,

I watched a boat bob an emerald wave. I'm less afraid. Less of a coward
than I was a year ago. Now, I am a checklist of risk. When I speak,

the words will not stop falling and this is what I ask before
every decision or task: Am I mechanism of gratification or need?

Am I more than what I feed? Indeed, are we not all an only child
with no sibling to blame? At Ezra's flat grave, covered in leaves,

I snap up a single shell curled on the slab. There have been no visitors
for a long while so I spray for bugs and the poisoned mist carries

over the dead. It is improper and a little funny and I say to myself,
"Stop spraying shit all over the poets." Even this fascist one.

The truth is I'd clear any grave. I want to redeem. To save.
That's my thing. My uselessness. A grim reaper too late. A retired priest.

Above, gulls chat and the cattle stars graze the sky. And at my eyeline,
insects stumble downwards, graceless, like unpardoned angels.

DEBT

There are graves
I owe visits to:

Alice and Teddy
and of course, Lindsey.

I tried to find
her headstone, buried up

in White Plains.
Only twenty when she died.

Now
when I meet

nineteen-year-olds
my heart hurts,

and I say a prayer.
Can't help it.

It's a habit.
I want to believe that everything

that has happened
is a lesson

but what could answer
to all that?

There are things
that are not forgivable

like when someone big
hurts someone small.

That's the only rule of nature
I believe in.

For that, you should burn.
For that, nothing can save you.

Once, Elisa talked a couple
in a fight

off the subway tracks
in Brooklyn.

Climbing back
onto the platform,

the guy pushed her
to the ground, told her

to mind her business,
and I still think

about that at 2 a.m.
when I'm in the mood

for murder.
She pulled her shoulder

in the fall.
Only a Sicilian

woman
could talk

two New Yorkers
out of their game

of chicken.
I bet they had

great sex that night
I joke,

and she takes
a long drag

of her cigarette
and says nothing.

PHOENIX

Why do I believe in any land that tells me it is holy?
Arizona, too, then, beckons in red, red rock
like Geryon's shoulder blades, plucked
on the first day of school. I pick up sand and throw it
like a half-committed ritual. A badly remembered
superstition. Like when my Catholicism meets
the land. Where am I supposed to be at this age?
Road ahead. Road behind. An ocean-flanked mind.
Back home, a gold wind slices the new york city night.
I mistake my loneliness for the suspended ribs of a bridge.
Can a rock have a follower? Can a low desert sky
follow me home? I start a cult for geographies
of the extremes and stick microphones into cacti arms,
record the juice and wind sound of its needles.
Wind is everything in the desert. More present than
a mirage or horizon. When we play back to hear
from the dead, we expect song. What we get
is a warning that goes on and on and on.

SAGITTARIUS

On the plane to Zurich, you tell me
you've recently moved your birthday to June.

When I ask, how does one move their birthday,
you say that you've always felt

you deserved to be born in summer.
While you're talking, I can't believe my luck

that we've been seated together at random
since I spotted you at the gate

and thought the drum in your ear
was beating faster than the world.

You say, I used to have psychological problems,
but now that's all settled, as if you've just closed

a deal on a house. When you pull out
a sleep mask, studded in blue rhinestones,

and announce your bedtime routine
while singing Prince, and everyone in our row

stares, I steady your giant box of cosmetics
and think, oh my god, I'm in love with you.

With anyone who can make a home of brevity
or insist on a new season for their birth.

Come see me in Vienna, you say. And I do.
Because I believe so much in being led.

IV

"I need to go backwards, to begin."

—MEENA ALEXANDER,
The Shock of Arrival

I DO EVERYTHING I'M TOLD

In Venice, there is always drama
around the corner and this city

is all corners and decay. You give me
that cathedral feeling and wipe rain

from blooms of jasmine shrubs
on my arm while I speak to Giovanni

about Italian boxing. That night,
I listen to Miguel on a terrace

while you fight with your boyfriend,
a chef, who doesn't want to meet me.

You show photos of his hands
with severed heads, black urchin shells,

a ripe sea egg. I nod at their dead beauty,
put on a playlist called

I do everything I'm told, and can't tell
what is kink or worship or both.

MAY TO DECEMBER

By August, we are sluggish with love. You slide two
barrettes into the night of my hair. Like twin fireflies.
Like rabbit feet dyed blue and downhearted, stamping
the side of my head. July's shadow is almost rot
and we haven't spoken in days. I play pool with Mik
and count the ways he sinks ball after ball while I await
the doom of going second, soon regret letting him break.
I bet on this game. I bet on the waning of light, fame. I know
most things dim. It's hot when I leave the bar and I say
come, sun, you muscular star, thinking heatstroke
might strike this state of weather from my heart.
The trigger of seasons, the treasons of these city streets.
Orchard and Broome. We loom. We make reasons and room
for why things can't work; we lurk into autumn.
We warm our hands for October's plume. We say soon, soon,
soon something will be revealed. We fool no one
and are no one's fool, least of all the late-summer gods
who know a burn, who rope in hope, who prepare us
for a meal of dead light. In August, I want snow. I want July.
Midsummer prophet sight. Belief. Faith. A cathedral
with all her weight. A winter love. A new year.
A regal infancy. A Sunday, born.

AUTUMN IN NEW YORK, 2020

Once upon a today, all land became sea and we,
an aquarium of the unclaimed. Yellow leaves sink
in the park pond, like orphan starfish, like mummies,
soft and eternal. My walk through this city is a riptide.
I hallucinate orcas and swim parallel to the rivers. Some days,
I hustle from the Hudson to the East, kick the fussed seagrass
dying in rectangular plots. The deadest blocks
of Manhattan are where sandwich chains
used to glow neon near the transit stations, places where
nothing happened except dread or anticipation or return.
Once upon a today, the city chewed herself like a dog
eating at its own leash, anchored to a desolate house.
I count each patch of park as I move south and do
a tour of the Lower East Side. I fall in love
with a rose building that was once a department store
where they sold velvet. And next to it, a German fabric shop
that sewed uniforms for those humans this country enslaved.
Once upon a summer, I only read Etheridge Knight
and asked a friend if she knew the history of her family wealth
when she sent her kid to private school on grandpa's money.
Once upon a season, I am a terrible dinner guest.
I get a cough. I take magnesium. I ingest chain link.
I want to call you and say that crisis clarifies everything,
but it hasn't. The world has gone milky and endangered
and I'm swallowing. I'm swallowing it all.

THE POET AND THE NURSE

A few days before it all unfolded in NYC,
a doctor was feeling my left breast
and we made jokes until we were not joking.

Go now, she said, because now was all
she could guarantee. I ducked awnings
forty blocks in the rainy blitz

of the March afternoon. I sat in an empty
hospital on 13th. There is a lump
with some debris another doctor told me

and I replied, *well, that doesn't sound very sexy*
because it wasn't. I went home and thought
about my rotting chest. My prophetic breast.

A week later, the same doctor who sent me
downtown closed her practice and learned
how to intubate patients on youtube.

Under lockdown, I sing cabaret by firelight.
And Helen in Paris is cooking fish
and chermoula in full Goth.

Alex makes a shopping list of champagne
and diet coke and audacity and says to me:
You better not look like shit at my funeral.

I dig my cast of macabre angels,
one foot in the grave, another on the internet.
When my sister calls me from Texas

after a long shift, I play piano for her
to forget her day, but I muddle keys.
They won't behave. She doesn't mind.

My sister has bathed and bagged the dead.
She is not tortured by a bad melody,
instead, she'd prefer pain not be

glamorous or candlelit or ironic
or theater. She knows that not everything
holy has to hurt or cohere.

THE FIRST OUTING

You bike blossoms to my apartment and I spray them down
as we ready for our long loop, masked with a man's length between us.

There is no rule except the one: *Keep this far apart,* the signs say in Central Park.
We stop by the Madonna Arch and Lorne Michaels bench, too. A hawk dives

at a nest of baby birds, already dead with lopped heads. Sparrows reign.
I piss on a rock. A solo trumpeter rips a song across the lake, the melody

running black. On a bench, a quote from *The Tempest.* Two lovers sit
under a bridge. Earlier, we stopped into Grand Central to gape

at the empty marble hall, the blue ceiling sketched gold with starlight
and for some reason, a medieval banquet came to mind with Lancelot

making speeches at court by the clock. All of time is mixed up.
On our way home through Times Square, godlike screens lap

for attention. Graveyard of capital. Techno–Mount Olympus. One giant
screen demands calm. Another, a guide for survival. The messages compete

for our brains: *If you have a fever . . . Bank of America is with you . . . Mask at all
times . . .*
One guy blasts A$AP Ferg and works out with a police barrier on the sidewalk.

What flex. He makes it all look so good. Like there is a way to swag your way
out of these circumstances. My friend who is a filmmaker once told me:

Excuse no one. That's what makes art, art.
So okay, I did it. I went for the walk.

I covered my face, but it was all unessential. It was just longing. To see others, sure,
but also, to stand at the mercy of the monuments that will outlive me.

BEGGARS AND CHOOSERS

"ah, Carl, while you are not safe, I am not safe."

—GINSBERG

I admit it. I don't really know how the internet works
or the economy and when the newspaper says
that the body of government is consolidating debt
to make room for more credit, it sounds like a divorce
or like when in-laws move in, this "making room,"
the language of spatial necessity escaping me.
I'm learning a lot about lungs in the pandemic:
glass opacity, x-rays of snow, organs embracing
like adjacent continents in a bad winter.
Mutual downfall. When I lived in Shanghai,
I performed a ritual of water to ward off a hoax
or a curse or the dead of heart. I needed an amulet
and bought an expensive piece of jade
because I was in China and I was desperate
and unimaginative. It was heavy, easily chipped.
I poured water into one glass and out of another.
I spoke to the horizontal incestuous gods— Apollo, Artemis, Athena.
I wished good things for you though now, a year later,
I want evidence that you, too, suffered, my generosity run dry
or maybe really wasn't there in the first place.
Under lockdown, you get so lonely that you begin
to personify furniture, and send me a video
of your body dancing with a ladder,
its long shadow cast wide against you.
I hate your audacious whimsy, bright as a smashing orange
against the sirens' howl. For every sick set of lungs
speeding by, your feet quicken around
the six-foot totem and I break,
envious of the inanimate, its stoic presence,
longing for any entanglement
with your form.

RETROSPECT

I think of my friend
often and again, today

ten minutes into a new year.
At the Odeon once,

I told him
he was easy to love

and he started to cry,
confessed no one

ever said that
before.

The truth
is that he could,

like all of us,
be hard

to love sometimes.
But he wasn't

that night.
Which is why I said it.

We sat in a red booth
and the glassware

made music
across the room

and everyone's face
blurred

into the fresh
current of spring.

MAGICAL REALISM IN AMERICA

for Eleutherius "Teddy" D'Souza

We made our childhood tree a kitchen
and a real estate office, a karate dojo
and a radio station. We rubbed wild chives
into pine needles and baked them until they
ran copper under the Pennsylvanian sun.
At night in the moonshine, my grandfather steers
his balcony from India to America and crosses two oceans
to descend to the land of this tree. He is tall,
and his gait, slow and methodical, looks as if
he's playing chess with air. He packs plastic cards
in his pocket and a note from my grandmother
to instruct me on my smart mouth. I offer him
our onion pines, our scallion trees. He puts down
a three of hearts and kisses Judith atop her head.
I tell him all the bad things I will do
when I am older and he sits, bony knees pointing,
one east, one west. *Remember the robin eggs*,
he asks and I am ashamed. I had taken them inside
and tried to hatch them with a hair dryer.
Blue, spotted oval planets. I held that dryer like a gun.
And when the yolk slipped through the crack,
I was devastated. Listen, I hate poems
about birds and grandparents and childhood friends.
I hate poems about birds and grandparents
and childhood friends almost as much
as I hate poems that break the fourth wall
like a cheeky high school play. It's just too easy.
But my grandfather's grave is in Goa and now Judith
has two kids so they must be summoned
somehow when I am terrible.
The three of us buried those sibling shells

under our childhood tree, the canopy just long enough
to cover my shame. No. The poem can't end here.
I'm sure he parted the branches and let in daylight.
Even sour light, he might say, is light.

you are all so dear to me. dearest. dear ones. one who endears and endures. dearful. deary. deary-eyed. downcast doll. i love you. i said it today. on a plane. i say it in all kinds of dreary weather. in london. i had an umbrella. it was extraordinary. sorry, this is a story. we get side-tracked. we like the sidetracks. we make wee cars and run them off tracks into long grass in a forest country(side). we slide into nature. we like the haunt of heaths. i reread wuthering heights. it's good. dear catherine. dearest heathcliff. my darlings. i put the characters to bed and get them up depending on what you have said. to me. that day. i wake daedalus. i wake augie march. i wake sula and zarathustra. they are my side tracks. they are the main road. dear megan. sorry, meg. small child inside me who cries *pass the sugar*, yes, here it is, stir it in, and who shall we wake today, my dear?

SONNET FOR THE UNBEARABLE

after Uvalde

If no ghost appears, it means too much is clear.
In the hazel woods, I went out at night
in search of it, the glow, and knelt at a grave
with grass unkempt and overstayed, and still
no spook came. It was a game. And then on
the screen, a shooting occurred, a school full
of tiny cubs who knew too few big words.
Those tufts of bear hair. I cried and washed
my grief in soap. A pink moon was foretold,
and tugged at my tides. My period arrived.
My heart's furnace went weak. No words. No speech.
The lord gives it all back, but there's a charge,
a charge for air so clear that no ghost appears.
There's no light to gossamer. No undead here.

ON YOUR DEPARTURE TO CALIFORNIA

Prayer for you out west. Where night falls
only after mine. The second curtain. That enigmatic dark
and daylight so clarifying, it hurts.
Prayer for the headless deer in Saratoga
and the thirty lobster shells we buried
in a small Connecticut town. For the elementary
school kids rushing headfirst into the Brooklyn twilight.
For the poets who came before and saw the purple
northeast, blizzard full, but no quakes, and wanted
for nothing else. For the gold shops of Jackson Heights,
and the dead soldiers in Mt. Auburn. For the dead
who just want to remain dead and not dance
into the speech of men. For the tiny churches
and their tiny bells. For every gas station. For the tri-states.
Yes, even for Jersey's ease. For Café Paulette, our last meal,
before the city fell. Prayer for our Hart Crane. For our bridge.
The blue one. For your return to Prospect Park
where I'll be waiting, smug, dripping in city bees.
Prayer for you, queen of the wide air, and your happy flights
and scraped-up knees and the young
fields behind you. Prayer for the sand-whipped
Rockaway Beach where we spent a birthday
and fought the wind. You ran into the cold May ocean
and I thought, "am I going to have to go in
if she gets caught?" just as you rose
from the water and waved.

MALAIKA

Means angel. Means angel, sorry I'm broke.
Means will you marry me anyway.
Is sung at every gathering in my family,
sometimes the elders just break into song
and all the kids roll their eyes or now
that everyone is dying, tentatively sing along
to the lyrics. Comes from Tanzania.
Is at home in the mouth of my father.
Was sung as we lowered my aunt in the fire.
Returns you to the earth. Means did I miss
my chance, sister. Means you disturb the heart.
Baby, you disturb my heart. Angel, it's you.

LOVE POEM

Sometimes, I wonder if I would know a beautiful thing if I saw it. So often, I was miserable when I was young, even in California with the ocean close and fat seals munching flatfish, tonguing urchins in their molars, sunning themselves pink by the sandy primrose. I ignored the whistle of the rock-faced mountain and her chorus of dry hills, walked past the blazing stars and lemons in dramatic ripe. I was so sad out west. The truth is I am most exquisite on the east coast, meaning I am in rhythm. I do not track the world by beauty but joy. That first bite into the soft carrot of tagine stew while a storm wailed over the East River. The misfit raccoon bouncing on trash bins in Central Park after we saw a Japanese play. We almost crashed a wedding that night at the Boathouse but lost our nerve. We were not dressed for the caper, but even this felt like rogue joy. Yes. It was joy, wasn't it? Even if it was ugly, it was joy.

NOTES

In "Reunion," the phrase "I am not a stupid child" is a line from Sandra Lim's poem "Certainty."

In "On Your Departure to California," the phrase "Queen of the wide air" is a line from a poem by John Keats called "I stood tip-toe upon a little hill."

The epigraph from "Rilke" is taken from "Orpheus, Eurydice, Hermes," translated from Rilke by Franz Wright.

The title "Dinner with Jack" refers to a conversation I had with Jack Halberstam.

The epigraph of the "Companion" comes from the Paul Schmidt's translation of Arthur Rimbaud's *A Season in Hell* with photographs by Robert Mapplethorpe. The book was published by Little, Brown and Company in 1998.

The ending line of "Companion" ("There's nothing at the bottom but a view") is a play on the title of the book by Tan Hoang Nguyen, *The View From the Bottom: Asian-American Masculinity and Sexual Representation*.

ACKNOWLEDGMENTS

The American Poetry Review: "Autumn in New York, 2020," "Beggars and Choosers," "Love Poem," "Magical Realism in America," and "The Poet and the Nurse"

Kenyon Review: Sonnets of the False Beloveds with One Exception, or Repetition Compulsion

Los Angeles Review of Books: "Do You Sell Dignity Here?" and "In Death, We Met in Scotland"

The Nation: "Orlando"

New England Review: "Letter to a Young Poet"

The New Yorker: "May to December" and "Shanghai"

Plume: "Paris Poem without Clichés"

Poetry: "Pound and Brodsky in Venice," "Reunion," "Semiotics," and "Winter"

TriQuarterly: "Catskills" and "How to Have Sex in Your Thirties (and Forties)"

PERSONAL ACKNOWLEDGMENTS

Thank you to the Yaddo Foundation, the Shanghai Swatch Art Peace Hotel Residency, and the Casa Ecco Residency in Lake Como for their support. I'd also like to thank the entire Tin House team, especially Alyssa Ogi.

This book found its thumping heart thanks to the insight of Adrian Matejka and Lisa Hiton who read the early manuscript. This book would not exist without the support of Egan Garr.

I'm grateful to have a big group of artists, thinkers, poets, and dreamers who were particularly important for this book including June, Jen, Lee, Mik, Rachelle, Dan, Randi, Alex, Kevin, Victoria, Jack, Marlies, Hala, Jeff, Edgar, the Paris crew, and so many more. You know who you are. Our conversations keep me curious about the world. Our intimacies house me when far from home. More adventures ahead, my loves.

Finally, thank you to Kevo, Mads, Judith, Mia, Micaela, and most especially, to Elisa and Josh. My life has been built from our years of laughter, meals, and untethered spontaneity. My love for you is without condition and does not know time. Lucky us.

© Rivkah Gevinson

MEGAN FERNANDES is the author of *Good Boys*, and a finalist for the Kundiman Poetry Prize and the Paterson Poetry Prize. Her poems have been published in *The New Yorker*, *Kenyon Review*, *The American Poetry Review*, *Ploughshares*, *The Common*, and the Academy of American Poets, among others. An associate professor of English and the writer-in-residence at Lafayette College, Fernandes lives in New York City.